WORLD ATLAS

by John Farndon

Silver Dolphin

San Diego, California

Silver Dolphin Books
An imprint of the Baker & Taylor Publishing Group
10350 Barnes Canyon Road, San Diego, CA 92121
www.silverdolphinbooks.com

Copyright ©2014 Studio Fun International, Inc.
44 South Broadway, White Plains, NY 10601 U.S.A. and
Studio Fun International Limited,
The Ice House, 124-126 Walcot Street, Bath UK BA1 5BG
All rights reserved.

Text copyright ©2014 Flowerpot Press
Designed by Flowerpot Press
Consultant: Richard Moore, MPA, Ph.D.

"Silver Dolphin" is a registered trademark of Baker & Taylor.
All rights reserved.

ISBN-13: 978-1-62686-303-3
ISBN-10: 1-62686-303-2

First published in the United States in 2000 by Copper Beech Books, an imprint of
The Millbrook Press, 2 Old New Milford Road, Brookfield, Connecticut 06804

Manufactured and printed in Shenzhen, China. Assembled in Hong Kong.
1 2 3 4 5 18 17 16 15 14
HH1/07/14 & HH3/07/14

CONTENTS

INTRODUCTION

Welcome to the wonderful world of maps! Each chapter examines a different region of our world, and each continent is explored in detail. Maps reveal each region's physical features, and highlight a few **cultural**, **economic**, and **political** points of interest. Each map also shows the flags of the nations, their capitals, and other major cities.

Mountain range

Accompanying text describes the region's countryside and points out individual physical features, such as the length of major rivers and the **altitude** of the highest mountains, to present a full view of the world's continents. Come along on a map adventure around the world!

Note: Words in **bold** are defined in the glossary.

Country
flag
and
name

Mountains

River

Country name

Capital city

Seas and oceans

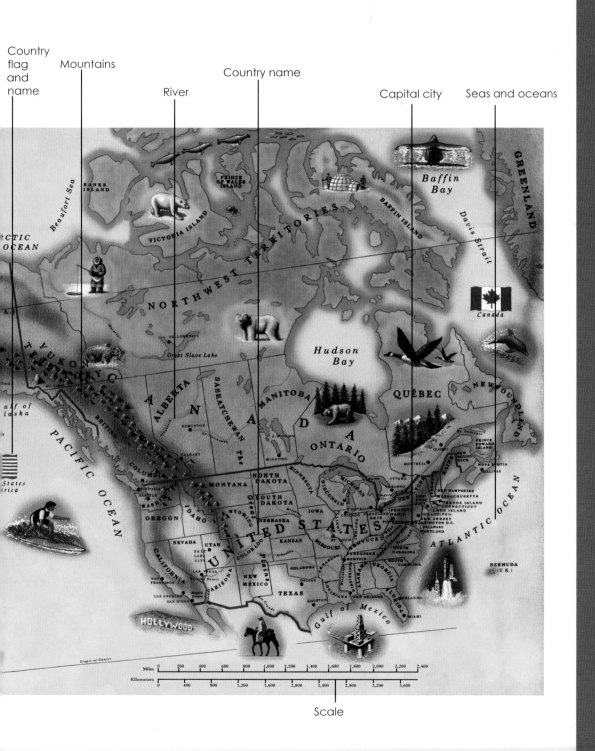

Scale

MAPS

Maps are one way we describe and **navigate** the world around us. Hikers use trail maps to find their way safely across mountains. **Surveyors** use city and county maps to know exactly who owns what land. Drivers use road maps to figure out how to get where they want to go. Meteorologists use **climate** maps to predict and show what weather is coming.

No matter who you are, where you are from, or what you are trying to do, there is a map that can give you the information you need to help you along the way.

One kind of world map is a globe. Globes are shaped like a ball—just like the planet Earth! When you look at a globe you can see the way the whole world looks. The sizes of countries are shown relative to each other. You can see how far apart countries are from each other and see the actual shapes of continents, since they don't have to be flattened out.

We each have our own way of looking at the world. Australia is known as "the Land Down Under," but do you think perhaps Australians think of the rest of the world as "the Lands Up Above"? When we each share our ideas with each other, the great big world seems a little more like home.

And that's something worth mapping out!

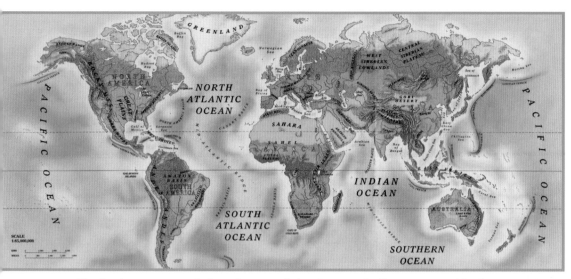

Physical maps reveal deserts, mountains, ice, and other geographical features. These maps almost never change.

Political maps show national borders, capitals, and names of countries. These maps change frequently.

NORTH AMERICA

The very north of North America is dominated by ice sheets and **tundra**. South of that lies a broad area of **boreal** forest, made up of **coniferous** trees. This gives way to broadleaf forests before reaching the massive prairies that lie at the heart of the continent.

The continent's highest peak, Mount McKinley, is found in Alaska and is 20,237 feet above sea level. It lies at the northern end of the Rocky Mountains, which stretch for 3,125 miles to New Mexico in the south. Evidence can still be found of these mountains' volcanic origins, such as the **geysers** in Yellowstone National Park, Wyoming. Running through the center of the continent is the Missouri-Mississippi river system, which snakes for 3,740 miles.

BANKS ISLAND

Beaufort Sea

ARCTIC OCEAN

Bering Strait

Arctic Circle

ALASKA (U.S.A.)

Yukon

Mt. McKinley

ANCHORAGE

YUKON TERRITORY

Mt. Lucas

ROCKY

Gulf of Alaska

KODIAK ISLAND

BRITIS

Alaska Peninsula

PACIFIC OCE

United States of America

Mount McKinley

Geyser, Yellowstone National Park

Tropic of Cancer

HAWAII (U.S.A.)

8

GREENLAND

Baffin
Bay

PRINCE
OF WALES
ISLAND

VICTORIA ISLAND

NORTHWEST TERRITORIES

BAFFIN ISLAND

Davis Strait

Canada

YELLOWKNIFE

Great Slave Lake

Hudson
Bay

QUÉBEC

NEWFOUNDLAND

ALBERTA

SASKATCHEWAN

MANITOBA

ONTARIO

A

N

A

D

A

EDMONTON

Athabasca

Saskatchewan

CALGARY

The

L. Winnipeg

WINNIPEG

St. Lawrence

QUÉBEC

PRINCE
EDWARD
ISLAND

NEW
BRUNS-
WICK

NOVA SCOTIA

HALIFAX

MONTRÉAL

COLUMBIA

VANCOUVER

VICTORIA

SEATTLE

WASHINGTON

OREGON

IDAHO

MONTANA

NORTH
DAKOTA

SOUTH
DAKOTA

MINNESOTA

Great

WISCONSIN

MICHIGAN

L. Superior

L. Huron

OTTAWA

TORONTO

Niagara
Falls

NEW YORK

MAINE

VERMONT

NEW HAMPSHIRE

MASSACHUSETTS

RHODE ISLAND

CONNECTICUT

LONG ISLAND

DETROIT

CLEVELAND

PITTSBURGH

NEW
YORK
CITY

PHILADELPHIA

NEW JERSEY

WASHINGTON D.C.

DELAWARE

MARYLAND

NEVADA

UTAH

SALT
LAKE
CITY

LAS VEGAS

WYOMING

COLORADO

NEBRASKA

IOWA

CHICAGO

ILLINOIS

INDIANA

OHIO

PENNSYL-
VANIA

ST. LOUIS

KENTUCKY

WEST
VIRGINIA

VIRGINIA

Missouri

Arkansas

KANSAS

MISSOURI

TENNESSEE

NORTH
CAROLINA

CALIFORNIA

SAN
FRANCISCO

LOS ANGELES

SAN DIEGO

Painted Desert

ARIZONA

Mojave
Desert

NEW
MEXICO

Rio Grande

OKLAHOMA

Plains

TEXAS

DALLAS

HOUSTON

ARKANSAS

MEMPHIS

Mississippi

LOUISIANA

ALABAMA

NEW ORLEANS

GEORGIA

SOUTH
CAROLINA

FLORIDA

ORLANDO

MIAMI

ATLANTIC OCEAN

BERMUDA
(U.K.)

UNITED STATES

HOLLYWOOD

Gulf of Mexico

Miles	0	200	400	600	800	1,000	1,200	1,400	1,600	1,800	2,000	2,200	2,400

Kilometers	0	400	800	1,200	1,600	2,000	2,400	2,800	3,600

NORTH AMERICA

Most of North America is occupied by its two largest countries: the United States and Canada. The United States is one of the most powerful countries in the world, and has many large cities, all kinds of modern **industries**, vast areas of **fertile** land, millions of cars, and the world's most successful television and film industry. Although most people speak English, there is a huge variety of peoples and climates in this land. In the south it is hot and tropical, in the west there are deserts, and the north is dotted with lakes and forests.

There are 50 states in the United States, including two that are separated from the rest. The islands of Hawaii are way out in the Pacific Ocean, and Alaska, the largest state of them all, is tacked onto the west of Canada.

Grand Canyon
Located in Arizona, this canyon is 277 miles long, up to 18 miles wide, and a mile deep! The Colorado River runs through the canyon, and is home to thousands of plant and animal species.

Statue of Liberty
This 305-foot statue stands on Liberty Island in New York Harbor. The people of France gave the statue to the United States in 1886 as a symbol of freedom and friendship.

Golden Gate Bridge
This orange suspension bridge stretches across San Francisco Bay. It connects San Francisco to California's northern counties, and has towers that are 746 feet tall.

10

Greenland is the largest island in the world. It is mostly rock, snow, and ice, though, and has a population of just 57,000 people. Greenland used to be ruled by Denmark, but now it has its own government.

Greenland

Canada is the second largest country in the world (after Russia). As in the United States, most people in Canada speak English, but in the province of Québec the primary language is French. Much of the country is made up of the cold and empty lands of the north, which stretch almost to the North Pole. All the main cities are in the south, close to the border with the United States—with which Canada shares the world's longest land border.

DID YOU KNOW?

The Niagara Falls are over 164 feet high and span a combined width of over 3,000 feet. The noise is incredible!

CN Tower
This observation tower in Toronto, Canada, is 1,814 feet tall. When it was built in 1976, it was the world's tallest tower, and today remains the largest freestanding structure in the Western Hemisphere.

CENTRAL and SOUTH AMERICA

North America's lower region, called Central America, connects it to South America. Central America's countryside changes from desert in the north of Mexico to lush, tropical **rain forest** that stretches from the Yucatan Peninsula all the way to South America. To the east is the Caribbean Sea, which is home to hundreds of islands. These lie in an arc from Cuba and the Bahamas in the north, to Trinidad and Tobago just off the coast of Venezuela.

South America contains one of the world's largest river systems. The Amazon winds for 4,073 miles from the Andes to the Atlantic. Its river basin covers 4.5 million square miles, has more than 200 **tributaries**, and is mostly covered in dense rain forest. South America also has the world's longest mountain chain, the Andes, stretching for 4,500 miles from Venezuela to Cape Horn.

ECUADOR

Ecuador

GALAPAGOS ISLANDS
(Ecuador)

Peru

Bolivia

Chile

Argentina

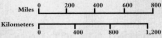

Paraguay

The Andes

Miles	0	200	400	600	800
Kilometers	0	400	800		1,200

ANGUILLA
ANTIGUA AND BARBUDA
ST. KITTS   GUADELOUPE
& NEVIS   DOMINICA
            MARTINIQUE
    ST. LUCIA BARBADOS
      ST. VINCENT & THE GRENADINES
GRENADA
        PORT OF SPAIN
        TRINIDAD & TOBAGO
        PARAMARIBO   CAYENNE
      GEORGETOWN   FRENCH
VENEZUELA GUYANA   SURINAM   GUIANA
RACAS
   Orinoco

Equator

A T L A N T I C   O C E A N

Colombia   French Guiana   Cuba   Bahamas

Dominican Republic   Jamaica

S. Francisco

BRAZIL

Amazon

Brazil

BRASILIA

Honduras   Costa Rica

Belize   Panama

Mato Grosso

Parana

RIO DE JANEIRO

Tropic of Capricorn

Antigua & Barbuda

P E R U

BOLIVIA

L. Titicaca

LIMA   LA PAZ

PARAGUAY

ASUNCION

Paraguay

A R G E N T I N A

Uruguay

URUGUAY

MONTEVIDEO

St. Kitts & Nevis   Dominica

Martinique   Barbados

St. Vincent & the Grenadines   Trinidad & Tobago

P A C I F I C

C H I L E

Atacama Desert

Mt Ojos del Salado

BUENOS AIRES

Pampas

Mt. Aconcagua

SANTIAGO

Uruguay

Venezuela

O C E A N

Patagonia

A T L A N T I C   O C E A N

El Salvador   Nicaragua

Haiti   Guatemala

Grenada

Guyana

FALKLAND ISLANDS
(U.K.)

St. Lucia

Strait of Magellan

N
W   E
S

Surinam

Tierra del Fuego

13

CENTRAL and SOUTH AMERICA

South America is generally a warm continent and lies across the equator. It includes the world's largest tropical rain forest, around the mighty Amazon River. Running down the west coast of South America is the world's longest mountain range, the Andes. High in these mountains the weather remains cool all year, and there are snowcapped peaks even at the equator.

The nations of Central America bask in a warm, tropical climate. To the east, scattered across the Caribbean Sea, lies a chain of islands sometimes called the West Indies. Many of these are tiny independent nations, such as St. Lucia and Grenada, famous for their beaches and warm blue seas.

The Americas were once **inhabited** by Native Americans, but in the 15th century European explorers arrived, followed by hundreds of European settlers, mainly from Spain. Now the main language of Central and South America is Spanish.

Amazon River
Considered the world's mightiest river, the Amazon is slightly shorter than the Nile in Africa. However, it contains far more water. In fact, one-fifth of the world's fresh water flows out of the Amazon River.

Machu Picchu
High in the Andes, this lost city was discovered again in 1911. The Incas built it in the 15th century as a royal estate for the emperor.

While Mexico is geographically part of North America, culturally it has more in common with the Central American countries than it does with the cultural traditions, language, and customs of North America. For this reason it is often grouped with the regions of Central and South America.

Chichen Itza
The ruins of one of the largest Mayan cities are located in what is now the Mexican state of Yucatan. The city was filled with many different types of architecture, and an estimated 1.2 million tourists visit it every year.

Angel Falls
In the South American country of Venezuela is the world's highest waterfall. Angel Falls, a thin ribbon of water falling 3,132 feet, was named after the man who discovered it, an American pilot named Jimmy Angel.

DID YOU KNOW?

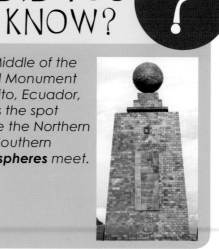

The Middle of the World Monument in Quito, Ecuador, marks the spot where the Northern and Southern **Hemispheres** meet.

Sweden

Norway

United Kingdom

Estonia

Latvia

ICELAND
• REYKJAVIK

Finland

FAROE ISLANDS

Denmark

Lake Onega

Lake Ladoga

HELSINKI

RUSSIAN

SHETLAND
ISLANDS

ORKNEY
ISLANDS

North Sea

DENMARK

Lake Vänern

Lake Vättern

STOCKHOLM

Baltic Sea

ST. PETERSBURG

TALLINN

ESTONIA

RIGA

LATVIA

MOSCOW

SCOTLAND

• EDINBURGH

NORTHERN
IRELAND

BELFAST

UNITED
KINGDOM

ENGLAND

AMSTERDAM

DUBLIN

REPUBLIC
OF IRELAND

Irish Sea

WALES

CARDIFF

LONDON

Elbe

BERLIN

GERMANY

POLAND

WARSAW

LITHUANIA

VILNIUS

BELARUS

MINSK

Russia

Vistula

KIEV

Dneper

UKRAINE

English Channel

NETHERLANDS

BRUSSELS

BELGIUM

LUXEMBOURG

Rhine

PRAGUE

CZECH
REPUBLIC

SLOVAKIA

BRATISLAVA

Dniester

MOLDOV

KISHINEV

Seine

PARIS

FRANCE

Loire

LIECHTENSTEIN

VADUZ

BERNE

SWITZERLAND

VIENNA

AUSTRIA

SLOVENIA

LJUBLJANA

Lake
Balaton

HUNGARY

BUDAPEST

ROMANIA

BUCHAREST

Black

Rhône

Alps

L. Geneva

Po

ZAGREB

CROATIA

Danube

BELGRADE

SERBIA

BULGARIA

SOFIA

ATLANTIC OCEAN

Bay of
Biscay

MONACO

Garonne

Pyrenees
Mts.

ANDORRA LA VELLA

ANDORRA

CORSICA

SAN MARINO

VATICAN
CITY
STATE

ROME

SARAJEVO

BOSNIA AND
HERZEGOVINA

Adriatic Sea

KOSOVO

TIRANA

MACEDONIA

SKOPJE

ALBANIA

ISTANBUL

ANKARA

TURKEY

GREECE

ATHENS

Aegean Sea

SPAIN

MADRID

PORTUGAL

Guadalquivir

LISBON

BALEARIC ISLANDS

SARDINIA

SICILY

PAROS

CRETE

NICOSIA

CYPRUS

Strait of Gibraltar

Malta

VALLETTA

MALTA

Greece

Mediterranean Sea

16

EUROPE

Europe, which includes a portion of Russia, covers about four million square miles.

The far north of the continent is dominated by tundra. To the south, the majority of the continent is taken up by the European plain, a large belt of fertile land, much of which has been turned over to farming. Farther south, the region is covered by shrubland.

Major European mountain chains include the Urals, which divide the continent from Asia; the Pyrenees between France and Spain; the Alps in central Europe; and the Carpathians to the east. Major rivers include the Rhine, the Rhône, the Danube, the Volga, and the Vistula.

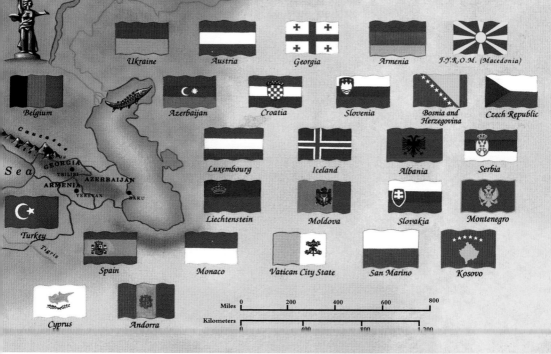

Belarus

Netherlands

Ireland

Portugal

Lithuania

Switzerland

Poland

FEDERATION

Italy

Ural Mountains

Germany

Romania

France

Hungary

Bulgaria

Volga

Ukraine

Austria

Georgia

Armenia

F.Y.R.O.M. (Macedonia)

Belgium

Azerbaijan

Croatia

Slovenia

Bosnia and Herzegovina

Czech Republic

Caucasus

Sea

GEORGIA

TBILISI

AZERBAIJAN

ARMENIA

YEREVAN

BAKU

Luxembourg

Iceland

Albania

Serbia

Turkey

Tigris

Liechtenstein

Moldova

Slovakia

Montenegro

Spain

Monaco

Vatican City State

San Marino

Kosovo

Cyprus

Andorra

Miles	0	200	400	600	800
Kilometers	0	400	800	1,200	

EUROPE

Europe can be divided into regions: western Europe, eastern Europe, and the hook-shaped tongue of land to the north known as Scandinavia. The weather is warm and sunny around the Mediterranean Sea, but becomes generally cooler the farther north you go. The northern part of Scandinavia is in the Arctic Circle, and winters here are long, dark, and bitterly cold.

Western Europe and Scandinavia are among the most **prosperous** parts of the world, with plenty of good farmland and modern industries that produce a wide range of products, including cars, medicines, clothing, and food.

Eastern Europe is similar in many ways, but its industries are older and the people are poorer. In recent years, however, countries such as Hungary, Poland, and Latvia have enjoyed new freedoms, and may soon become as prosperous as the countries of western Europe.

Neuschwanstein Castle
Located in the south of Germany, this castle looks like something from a fairy tale. Named the top tourist attraction in Germany, it was built by King Ludwig II as a personal retreat when he lost his throne to the Prussians in 1866.

St. Basil's Cathedral
This former church, located in Moscow, Russia, was built by Ivan the Terrible in 1555. Its stunning architecture makes it immediately recognizable.

Paris, the capital of France, is a magnificent sight! The domed church of Sacre Coeur, the cathedral of Notre Dame, the amazing Arc de Triomphe, and the huge metal Eiffel Tower, designed by the great French engineer Alexander Eiffel over 100 years ago, all make Paris the beautiful and memorable city it is today.

Eiffel Tower

Stonehenge
This prehistoric stone monument in southern England is one of the wonders of the world. We don't know who built Stonehenge, or why—or how people were able to move the massive stones before machines were invented!

Colosseum
This giant amphitheater is in the center of Rome, Italy. It was built in the first century.

Little Mermaid statue
This bronze statue of a mermaid, based on the fairy tale by Hans Christian Andersen, is displayed on a rock along the promenade in Copenhagen, Denmark.

Morocco

Tunisia

Mauritania

Israel

Lebanon

Syria

Egypt

Jordan

MADEIRA
FUNCHAL

CANARY ISLANDS
(Spain)

OCEAN

ATLANTIC

Atlas Mountains

RABAT

ALGIERS

TUNIS

TUNISIA

Mediterranean Sea

TRIPOLI

Algeria

Libya

Libyan Desert

SYRIA

BEIRUT
LEBANON

DAMASCUS
AMMAN

JERUSALEM

ISRAEL
JORDAN

CAIRO

Nile

Red Sea

MOROCCO

EL AAION

WESTERN
SAHARA

ALGERIA

LIBYA

EGYPT

Sahara Desert

CHAD

MAURITANIA
NOUAKCHOTT

MALI

NIGER

Niger

Sudan

ERITREA

THE
GAMBIA
BANJUL

SENEGAL

DAKAR

GUINEA

Niger

BAMAKO

OUAGADOUGOU

NIAMEY

Niger

Lake
Chad

N'DJAMENA

KHARTOUM

SUDAN

Blue Nile

BISSAU

GUINEA
BISSAU

CONAKRY

FREETOWN

BURKINA FASO

CENTRAL
AFRICAN REPUBLIC

SOUTH
SUDAN

ADDIS
ABABA

ETHIOPIA

SIERRA LEONE

MONROVIA

CÔTE
D'IVOIRE

GHANA

YAMOUSSOUKRO

TOGO

BENIN

NIGERIA

ABUJA

LAGOS

LIBERIA

ACCRA

PORTO
NOVO

LOME

EQUATORIAL GUINEA

SAO TOME

CAMEROON

YAOUNDE

BANGUI

DR CONGO

UGANDA

KAMPALA

KENYA

NAIROBI

Senegal

Ghana

Burkina Faso

MALABO

LIBREVILLE

SAO
TOME
&
PRINCIPE

GABON

BRAZZAVILLE

R CONGO

KIGALI

RWANDA

BUJUMBURA

BURUNDI

Lake
Victoria

ZANZI

TANZANIA

DODOMA

Gambia

ASCENSION

Nigeria

ATLANTIC

KINSHASA

LUANDA

Democratic Republic
of the Congo

Guinea-Bissau

Côte d'Ivoire

ST HELENA

ANGOLA

ZAMBIA

LILONGWE

Lake
Nyasa

MALAWI

MOZAMBIQUE

Guinea

Liberia

LUSAKA

Sierra Leone

Mali

Togo

Tropic of
Capricorn

NAMIBIA

HARARE

ZIMBABWE

BOTSWANA

WINDHOEK

GABORONE

PRETORIA

MAPUTO

MBABANE

SWAZILAND

Benin

Gabon

SOUTH AFRICA

MASERU

LESOTHO

Cameroon

Equatorial Guinea

Cape of
Good
Hope

AFRICA and the MIDDLE EAST

African savanna

Africa covers 22 percent of the earth's land area—about 11.7 million square miles. The northern half of the continent is dominated by the Sahara Desert. To the south is the area of grassland called the "Sahel." The continent's center contains the Congo River basin and the rain forest.

To the east are the Serengeti and the Great Rift Valley. These are a series of cracks in the earth that have formed steep-sided valleys.

Major rivers include the Niger, the Congo, and the Nile, which stretches for 4,130 miles. Major mountain chains include the Atlas Mountains and the Ethiopian Highlands. The highest point is Mount Kilimanjaro in Tanzania, which is 19,340 feet high.

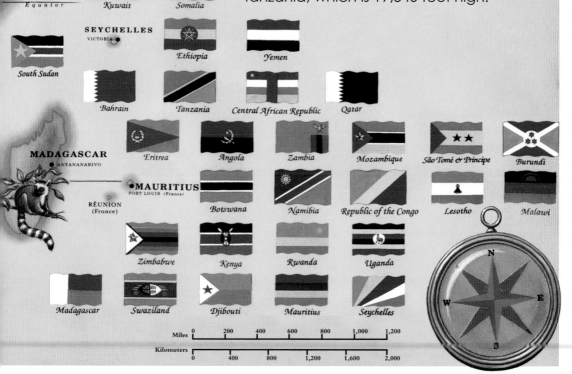

Iraq

Iran

IRAN

BAHRAIN

QATAR

UNITED ARAB EMIRATES

SAUDI ARABIA

OMAN

YEMEN

SOMALIA

INDIAN OCEAN

Oman

United Arab Emirates

Saudi Arabia

Kuwait

Somalia

SEYCHELLES

Ethiopia

Yemen

South Sudan

Bahrain

Tanzania

Central African Republic

Qatar

MADAGASCAR

Eritrea

Angola

Zambia

Mozambique

São Tomé & Príncipe

Burundi

MAURITIUS

RÉUNION (France)

Botswana

Namibia

Republic of the Congo

Lesotho

Malawi

Zimbabwe

Kenya

Rwanda

Uganda

Madagascar

Swaziland

Djibouti

Mauritius

Seychelles

Miles	0	200	400	600	800	1,000	1,200
Kilometers	0	400	800	1,200	1,600	2,000	

AFRICA and the MIDDLE EAST

The Middle East lies on the eastern end of the Mediterranean Sea and is an important crossroads for trade between Europe, Africa, and Asia. These days one of its main trading products is oil. Dubai has become a global city and business hub of the Middle East and Persian Gulf.

Dubai

South of the Mediterranean Sea lies the great Sahara Desert, and beyond that all the countries of the rest of Africa—a vast and varied region of tropical forest, grassland, mountains, and desert.

Sahara Desert

The Pyramids lie just outside of Cairo, the capital of Egypt. They were built as tombs for ancient Egyptian kings. There are passages and small rooms inside the Pyramids, but mostly they are just stone.

The Pyramids

Victoria Falls
This waterfall, on the border of Zambia and Zimbabwe in southern Africa, is known as the greatest curtain of falling water in the world. Also called "Mosi-oa-Tunya" (meaning "the smoke that thunders"), its spray can be seen from miles away.

DID YOU KNOW?

Africa is one of the most varied parts of the world. It has 52 independent countries—more than any other continent.

Mount Kilimanjaro
Located in Tanzania, this is the highest mountain in Africa and the highest freestanding mountain in the world. At 19,341 feet above sea level, it is very cold at the top, even though it is close to the equator.

NORTHERN ASIA

Northern Asia is covered in tundra. Below this lies a large band of boreal forest, or **taiga**. Sitting in the center of Asia is the Gobi Desert, which covers 500,000 square miles. Surrounding this dry area are wide tracts of grasslands, known as steppes.

Major rivers include the Volga and the Chang (Yangtze), which is 3,915 miles long. The eastern coast of Asia sits on the edge of what is known as the Ring of Fire, so named for volcanic activity that over millions of years has created peaks such as Mount Fuji in Japan.

Gobi Desert

BARENTS SEA

Kara Sea

RUSSIAN FEDERATION

Yenisey

Ob

NOVOSIBIRSK

OMSK

Irtysh

Ural Mountains

Volga

Ural

MOSCOW

KAZAKHSTAN

Lake Balkhash

ALMA-ATA

Takliman (Desert)

BISHKEK

KYRGYZSTAN

Aral Sea

UZBEKISTAN

TASHKENT

Pamir

Caspian Sea

Karakum Desert

DUSHANBE

TURKMENISTAN

TAJIKISTAN

ASHGABAT

Mountains

Himalayas

Tajikistan

Mac

Laptev Sea

East Siberian Sea

Bering Strait

Arctic Circle

RUSSIAN FEDERATION

YAKUTSK •

Russian
Federation

Lena

Sea of
Okhotsk

PACIFIC OCEAN

Mongolia

Trans-Siberian Railway

North Korea

IRKUTSK •
Lake Baikal

Hokkaido

VLADIVOSTOK •

Honshu

Japan

South Korea

ULAN BATOR •

MONGOLIA

Gobi Desert

NORTH KOREA

PYONGYANG •

SEOUL •

Mt. Fuji

TOKYO •

JAPAN

BEIJING •

SOUTH
KOREA

Shikoku

Taiwan

Turkmenistan

Great Wall of China

Huang He

Yellow Sea

Sea of Japan

Kyushu

SHANGHAI •

East China
Sea

Tropic of Cancer

Kazakhstan

Kyrgyzstan

Chang Jiang (Yangtze)

CHINA

• Taipei
Taiwan

MACAU •

HONG KONG •

Hong Kong

Uzbekistan

China

| Miles | 0 | 200 | 400 |
| Kilometers | 0 | 400 | 800 |

N
W E
S

NORTHERN ASIA

Siberia, the name for almost all of the Asian part of Russia, is a vast region, one and a half times the size of the United States. Siberia is famous for its icy northern areas, but the region is also rich in oil and gas. There are very few people here, except in the large industrial cities along the course of the Trans-Siberian Railway.

Trans-Siberian Railway

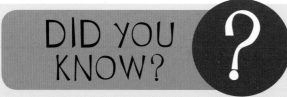 DID YOU KNOW?

The Chinese people began to build parts of the Great Wall as early as the fifth century BC, and construction continued for 21 centuries. It is now 13,170 miles long!

Much of China is also sparsely populated, for huge areas are occupied by cold desert and high mountains. But China has over 1.35 billion people, giving it the largest population in the world. China has numerous industries, making everything from shoes to cars.

Just a little farther east, however, is the world's most successful industrial nation: Japan. The bullet train (or Shinkansen), which travels at speeds of 150 to 200 miles per hour around Japan, is considered one of the fastest and safest railroad systems in the world.

Forbidden City
Located in the center of Beijing, China, this site was home to Chinese royalty for over 500 years. It has 980 buildings and now houses the Palace Museum.

Bullet train

Mount Fuji
The highest mountain in Japan, Mount Fuji is 12,388 feet tall. It is also an active volcano that last erupted in 1708. Mount Fuji is located on Honshu Island, about 62 miles southwest ot Tokyo, and can be seen from there on a clear day.

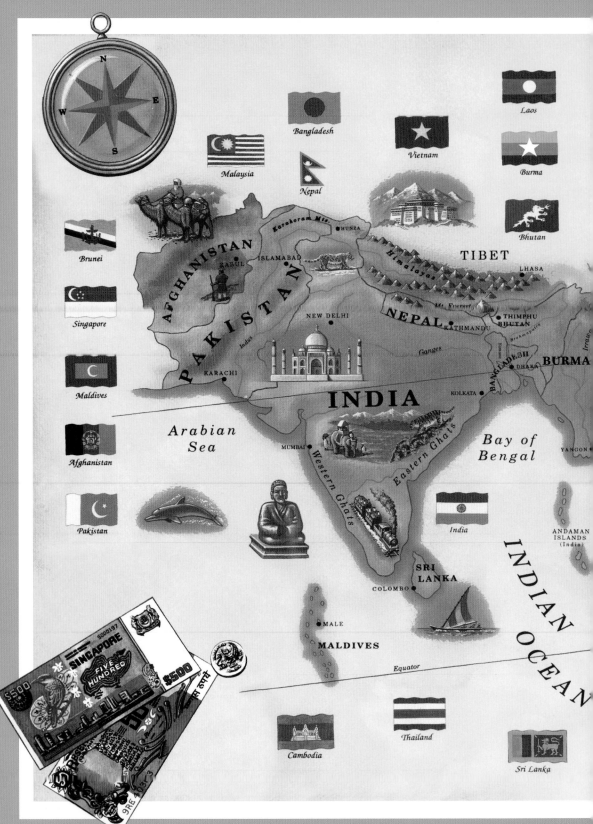

Bangladesh

Laos

Vietnam

Burma

Malaysia

Nepal

Brunei

Bhutan

Singapore

Maldives

Afghanistan

Pakistan

Karakoram Mts.   HUNZA

TIBET

LHASA

AFGHANISTAN

KABUL ISLAMABAD

Himalayas

Mt. Everest

NEW DELHI

NEPAL   THIMPHU
KATHMANDU BHUTAN

P A K I S T A N

Indus

Ganges

Brahmaputra

Irrawaddy

BANGLADESH
DHAKA

BURMA

KARACHI

INDIA

KOLKATA

Arabian
Sea

MUMBAI

Eastern Ghats

Bay of
Bengal

YANGON

Western Ghats

India

ANDAMAN
ISLANDS
(India)

SRI
LANKA

COLOMBO

INDIAN OCEAN

MALE

MALDIVES

Equator

Thailand

Cambodia

Sri Lanka

28

SOUTH and SOUTHEAST ASIA

South and Southeast Asia are lush and fertile places. Apart from the desert area in western Pakistan and the scrublands of central India, the region is rich in farmland and tropical vegetation.

The major rivers include the Ganges, which flows from the Himalayas to the Indian Ocean at Bangladesh, and the Mekong, which is 2,703 miles long.

The major mountain chain in this region is called the Himalayas. They contain most of the world's highest peaks, including Mount Everest, which is 29,028 feet high. The region of sea between the Pacific and Indian Oceans is filled with thousands of islands—Indonesia alone includes more than 13,600 islands.

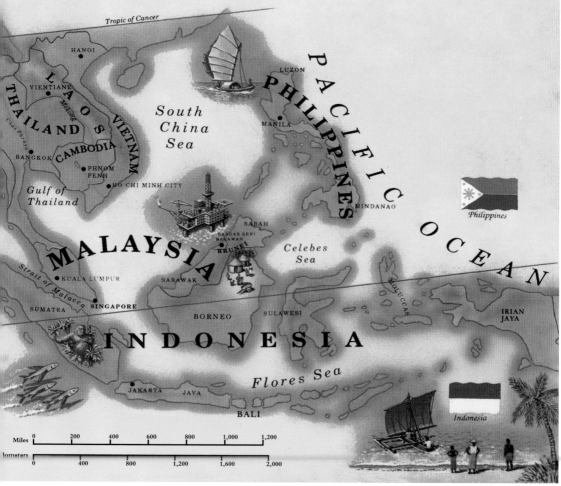

SOUTH and SOUTHEAST ASIA

The region called Southeast Asia includes the thousands of islands of Indonesia and the Philippines, which lie scattered over the warm, tropical seas. The rest of Southeast Asia forms part of the mainland. Most of the people live by farming, but the region also has numerous new industries, producing such things as electronics, cars, clothes, and toys.

Farther west lies the great diamond-shaped country of India, with Pakistan and Bangladesh sitting at either side. India has one of the largest populations of any country in the world, and many of its people live in sprawling industrial cities, such as Bombay and Calcutta. The landscape varies from the hot, dusty plains in the center of the country to the cool mountains of the north, which reach up toward the mighty, snowcapped Himalayas. India's weather is generally hot and dry, but in the **monsoon** season it can rain heavily for weeks.

India has over 850 million people (the second-largest population in the world after China), at least five religions, 14 official languages, and over 1,000 other languages!

Taj Mahal
Meaning "crown of palaces," the Taj Mahal is a white marble mausoleum located in Agra, India. With precious gems and stones embedded in the marble, the building appears to be pink in the morning, white during the day, and golden in the evening.

Banaue Rice Terraces
These are 2,000-year-old rice terraces, carved into the mountains in the Philippines by hand. The terraces are built 5,000 feet above sea level, and are still used today for growing rice and vegetables.

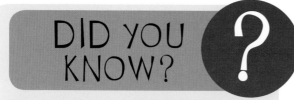

DID YOU KNOW?

Mount Everest was first climbed in 1953 by the New Zealander Sir Edmund Hillary, and Tenzing Norgay from Nepal. Since then, several thousand climbers have been to the top—and over a hundred have been killed trying to do so.

Angkor Wat
Meaning "temple city," Angkor Wat is the largest religious monument in the world. It is a temple complex in Cambodia that was built in the 12th century.

Papua New Guinea

Solomon Islands

IRIAN JAYA

PAPUA
NEW
GUINEA

SOLOMON
ISLANDS

PORT
MORESBY

Coral Sea

*Gulf of
Carpentaria*

DARWIN

Great Barrier Reef

The Great Dividing Range

INDIAN OCEAN

NORTHERN
TERRITORY

QUEENSLAND

*Great Sandy
Desert*

AUSTRALIA

*Simpson
Desert*

ALICE
SPRINGS

*Gibson
Desert*

Ayers Rock

BRISBANE

WESTERN AUSTRALIA

*Great Victoria
Desert*

*Great Artesian
Basin*

NEW SOUTH WALES

Darling

SOUTH
AUSTRALIA

SYDNEY

CANBERRA

Mt. Kosciusko

PERTH

Great Australian Bight

ADELAIDE

Murray

VICTORIA

SOUTHERN OCEAN

MELBOURNE

Bass Strait

Australia

TASMANIA

HOBART

Western Samoa

Miles	0		200		400		600		800

	0		400		800		1,200

AUSTRALIA and the PACIFIC ISLANDS

The country of Australia is the world's smallest continent, covering almost 3 million square miles. The majority of the country's interior is covered in scrub and desert, notably the Great Sandy and the Great Victoria Deserts. To the north, the climate is more tropical, supporting lush rain forest. Running north to south along the eastern edge of the country is the Great Dividing Range. At the southern end of this range is the continent's highest point, Mount Kosciusko, which is 7,316 feet high. The longest river is the Murray-Darling system, at nearly 2,300 miles long. New Zealand's climate is far cooler than Australia's—its southern coast is similar to the **fjord** landscape of northern Europe. The Pacific Ocean is home to hundreds of tiny islands, such as those of Western Samoa.

AUSTRALIA and the PACIFIC ISLANDS

If you stuck all the land on the earth together, it would still be smaller than the Pacific Ocean—that's how big the world's largest ocean is. It is dotted with hundreds of tiny islands, including some of the world's smallest independent nations, such as Nauru and Tonga. The largest islands of the region are all in the southwest. New Guinea is one of the largest islands in the world. It is now divided into two halves: Papua New Guinea (an independent country) and Irian Jaya (a part of Indonesia).

New Guinea coast

Ayers Rock
Also called Uluru, Ayers Rock is a large sandstone rock formation in central Australia that looks bright red at sunrise and sunset. The 1,142-foot-high rock is sacred to the Anagu, the Aboriginal people of the area.

Australia is so big that it is called a continent. Although Aborigines have lived there for over 40,000 years, modern Australia was founded by Europeans who settled there in the late 18th century. Australia's landscape is dominated by the Outback, a region of deserts and semi-arid land. Like Australia, New Zealand has a large European population and its main language is English. New Zealand is largely mountainous. Its glaciers are a result of its high elevations and cool, wet air.

Franz Josef Glacier
This glacier is more than seven miles long and is located in Westland Tai Poutini National Park on the west coast of New Zealand's South Island. Today, visitors can take a helicopter ride up to the glacier to walk, hike, or enjoy the natural hot pools there.

DID YOU KNOW?

John Utzon, the Danish architect who designed the Sydney Opera House, won an international design competition for his plans in 1957.

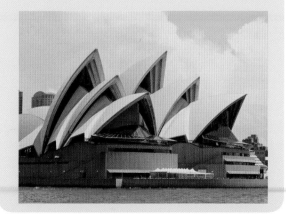

Mount Eden Crater
Also called Maungawau, this crater is a volcanic cone in the Auckland region of New Zealand. A volcano erupted 15,000 years ago from three overlapping cones and formed a huge mound with a central crater from the last eruption.

ANTARCTICA

During the winter months (June, July, and August) it is totally dark for weeks on end. The only people living here are scientists studying the weather, the polar ice cap, and the wildlife, which includes the various kinds of penguins and seals that live around the edge of the continent.

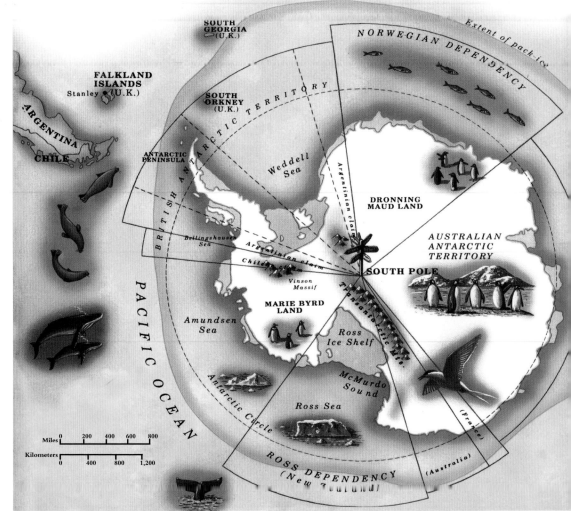

This continent, including the ice cap that stretches into the Southern Ocean in many places, covers about 5,468,750 square miles. The ice sheet has an average thickness of about 6,800 feet, and can reach 14,800 feet deep.

Antarctica is also the place where the world's lowest natural temperature was recorded—an astonishing –128.6°F. Normally, the temperature rarely reaches above freezing. Antarctica has no rivers, but has mountain chains such as the Transantarctic Mountains; the highest point, the Vinson Massif, is 15,900 feet high.

Transantarctic Mountains
The Transantarctic Mountains are a range in Antarctica that divides East Antarctica and West Antarctica.

Emperor penguins
Emperor penguins breed on the winter ice surrounding Antarctica. The female lays a single egg, which the male keeps warm by standing over it for about two months while the female goes to get food.

THE ARCTIC

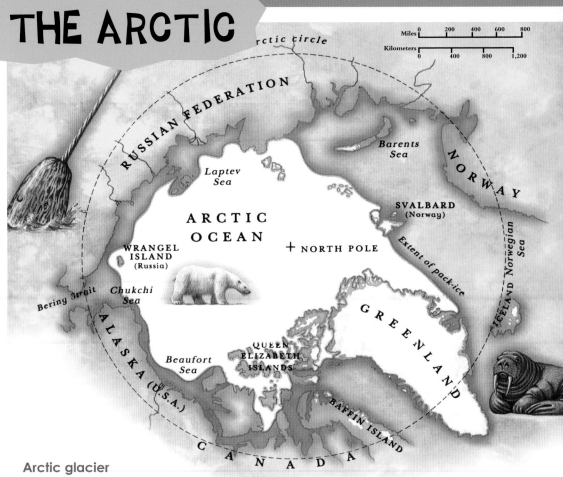

Arctic circle

| Miles | 0 | 200 | 400 | 600 | 800 |
| Kilometers | 0 | 400 | 800 | 1,200 |

RUSSIAN FEDERATION

Barents Sea

NORWAY

Laptev Sea

SVALBARD (Norway)

ARCTIC OCEAN

+ NORTH POLE

Extent of pack-ice

WRANGEL ISLAND (Russia)

ICELAND

Norwegian Sea

Bering Strait

Chukchi Sea

ALASKA (U.S.A.)

Beaufort Sea

QUEEN ELIZABETH ISLANDS

GREENLAND

BAFFIN ISLAND

C A N A D A

Arctic glacier

The region known as the Arctic consists of the Arctic Ocean and numerous islands, including Greenland and Wrangel Island—there is no single continental **landmass**. The North Pole sits in the center of this frozen ocean. The Arctic Ocean, the world's smallest ocean, covers about 5,440,000 square miles, and most of this lies under ice throughout the year. This pack ice increases in size during the winter months, when most of the region is in darkness while the sun remains below the horizon. This is because the earth spins around the sun at an angle, keeping the North Pole in shade during the winter months. Beyond the ice sheet, the surrounding islands are covered with a tundra landscape, which frequently blooms with flowers during the milder summer months.

Conditions here are among the harshest on earth. In midwinter, it is dark 24 hours a day, the temperature can drop below –58°F, and freezing winds blast the barren landscape. Despite this, many animals live here. Polar bears and Arctic foxes are active all year, hunting on the large, moving ice floes. Arctic hares and lemmings burrow in the snow to escape the winter weather. Other animals migrate. The ice sheet shrinks as temperatures rise. Snow melts to reveal the tundra (land where trees cannot grow), and the lower soil is always frozen. But hardy flowers grow and attract insects, which bring out herbivores, such as reindeer, and predators, like wolves.

Polar bear
The polar bear is a powerful swimmer that hunts on the ice floes. Stalking its prey on the ice, it is camouflaged by its coat, and the hairy soles of its feet keep it from slipping.

Arctic fox
The fur of the Arctic fox is gray or brown in the summer, but turns white in the winter to match its surroundings, so it can hunt and **scavenge** without being seen.

Snow geese
Snow geese are not always white—they can be blue or gray. They fly north each spring to breed in the short Arctic summer, where they have virtually no predators or competitors. Snow geese pair for life and raise their young together.

SEAS and OCEANS

The seas and oceans around the world hold 96 percent of the world's water, and cover over two-thirds of the planet's surface. The largest ocean, the Pacific, covers 63.8 million square miles. The deepest point in the oceans is the Marianas Trench in the Pacific. It is nearly seven miles deep.

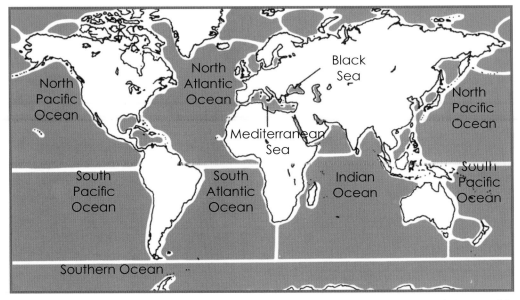

Seas and oceans of the world

The seas hold an amazing range of life. Coral reefs, found off the coasts of Australia, Central America, and Africa, are home to animals ranging from tiny corals to clams, stingrays, and an array of brightly colored fish. Life in the deep ocean includes **microscopic** plankton. These tiny organisms form the basic food supply for others, from crabs to enormous whales.

Coral reef

Surrounding a landmass is a shallow part of the sea called the continental shelf. At about 60 miles from the shore, the seafloor drops off sharply down the continental slope, before arriving at the ocean floor about four miles below the surface.

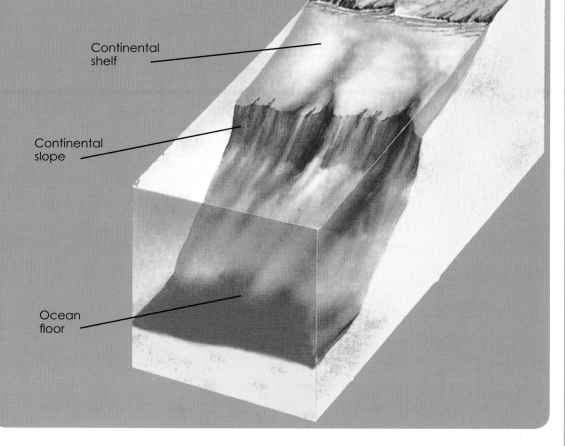

Continental shelf

Continental slope

Ocean floor

Coastal erosion
The powerful forces of the seas and oceans can have devastating effects on the rocks and soil of the coastline, eroding huge amounts from some areas and depositing them in others. The results can be stunning, with such formations as the enormous rock stacks of the Twelve Apostles on Australia's south coast.

MOUNTAINS

Mountains and hills have been formed over millions of years as the earth has shifted, causing areas to be crumpled up into jagged peaks, such as the Himalayas. They may also be the result of volcanic activity, and today, many chains of mountains still have active volcanoes, such as Mount St. Helens in Washington state.

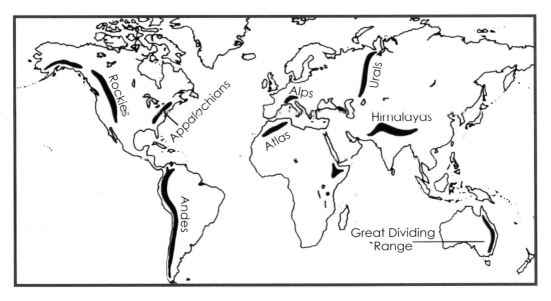

Mount St. Helens

Sharp mountains
Sharp mountain peaks are signs of a young mountain range that has not been eroded to a great extent.

Smooth mountains
Smoother mountains indicate an old mountain range. This is because they have been eroded to their present shape.

Mountain wildlife has to cope with harsh environments. Few large and ornate plants can survive the unpleasant conditions. Instead, the plants tend to be small and low-growing. Mountain animals must adapt to survive. The bighorn sheep of the Rocky Mountains have thick fur and are sure-footed climbers.

As the climate changes with altitude on a mountain slope, different types of plants will grow at different heights.

Plant Altitudes

1 At the top of the highest peaks are snow and ice, where little grows.

2 Below this is a strip of alpine meadow, containing some flowering plants and grasses.

3 The highest trees are found in the band of coniferous evergreen forest.

4 These are followed by **deciduous** trees (ones that shed their leaves).

5 If the climate is warm and wet enough, next is tropical cloud forest.

6 These are followed by more bands of deciduous trees.

7 Finally, there are bands of evergreen trees.

8 These give way to open grassland at the foot of the mountain.

FORESTS

Large areas of land on almost every continent, with the exception of Antarctica, are covered in forests of one kind or another. These can be the enormous boreal forests that stretch across the northern regions of North America, Asia, and Europe, or the concentrations of rain forest that fill the centers of South America and Africa. These great areas of land are under threat from massive deforestation programs that clear forests at an alarming rate—over 50,000 square miles each year.

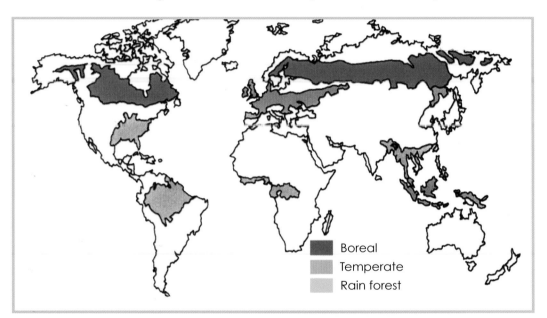

- Boreal
- Temperate
- Rain forest

Wolf
The European wolf travels in small packs that hunt together for livestock or even garbage! Though they were almost **extinct** at one point, they are now growing at a steady rate.

Pine marten
The large paws and sharp claws on the pine marten help it grip branches as it climbs trees. It also uses its long, bushy tail for balancing.

The large region of woodland stretching across Russia and Siberia is the largest forest on the planet. It ranges for over 6,250 miles from the Baltic Sea in the west to the Pacific Ocean in the east.

One of the most diverse and richly populated forms of environment, rain forests are found in the warmer and wetter parts of the world, such as South America, central Africa, and Southeast Asia. The rich growing conditions ensure the growth of a huge variety of plants that can support a wide diversity of animal life. These animals range from tigers to brightly colored birds, such as the toucan.

Rain forest

Toucan
There are 34 different species of toucans. Some have a beak as long as their body!

DESERTS

Although deserts are generally thought of as hot areas, the term applies to any region with very little rainfall. Deserts cover about 14 percent of the earth's land area, the largest being the Sahara in North Africa. Of these deserts, only 10 to 20 percent are actually covered in sand.

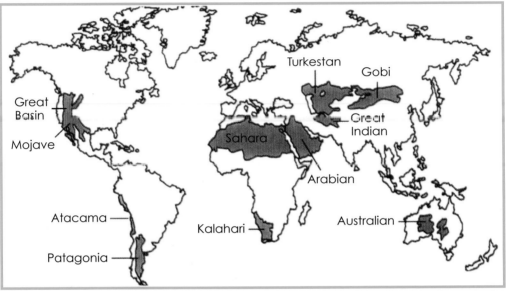

Turkestan

Gobi

Great Basin

Mojave

Great Indian

Sahara

Arabian

Atacama

Kalahari

Australian

Patagonia

Deserts of the world

Creatures that live in the desert have developed special physical features and behaviors that suit the harsh climate. Camels have large, padded feet to stop them from sinking into the sand, and long eyelashes to stop sand from being blown into their eyes. The fennec fox has large ears to help it stay cool. Desert lizards need the warm weather to survive. However, too much heat can be fatal. To escape the harsh sun, the lizard burrows into the cool ground.

Desert lizard

Fennec fox

Camel

Sand dunes
Dunes are formed by wind blowing over sand in the same way that wind causes waves when it blows over water. Sand dunes can be up to 1,525 feet high and three miles long.

Some deserts, such as the Atacama in South America, are called rain-shadow deserts. They are usually found behind a chain of mountains. As warm, moist air blows into the mountain chain, it rises and cools. As it cools, the air is unable to hold onto its water, which forms clouds and then falls as rain. As the now-dry air passes over the mountains, it falls and gets warmer, creating a warm, dry area, or rain-shadow zone.

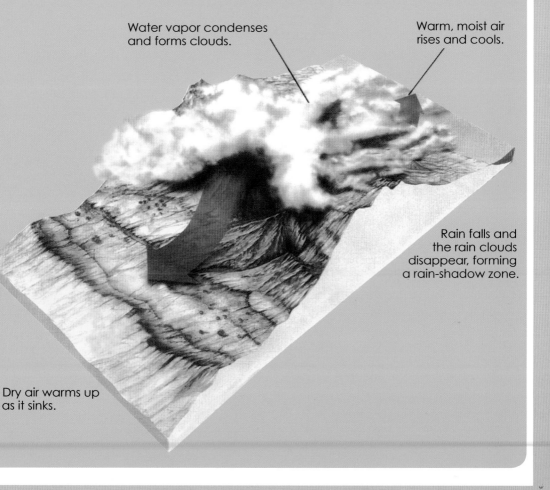

Water vapor condenses and forms clouds.

Warm, moist air rises and cools.

Rain falls and the rain clouds disappear, forming a rain-shadow zone.

Dry air warms up as it sinks.

PHYSICAL MAP of the WORLD

Physical maps show us the natural features of the earth, such as the locations and names of oceans, mountains, rivers, and deserts.

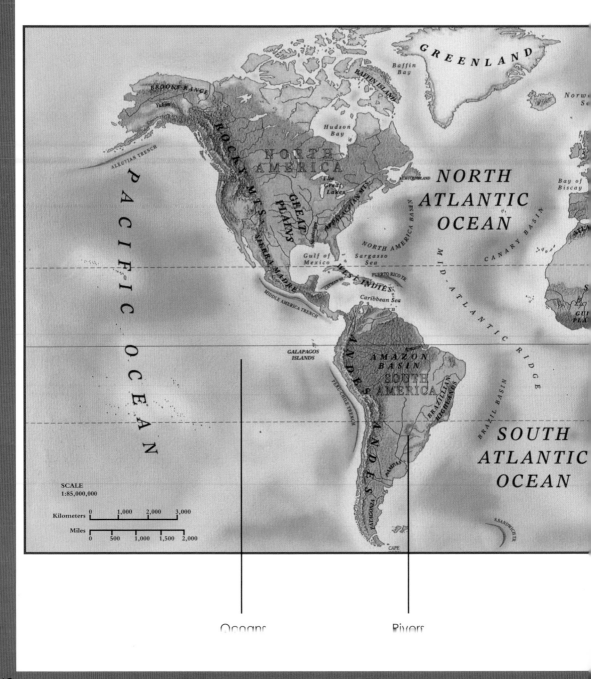

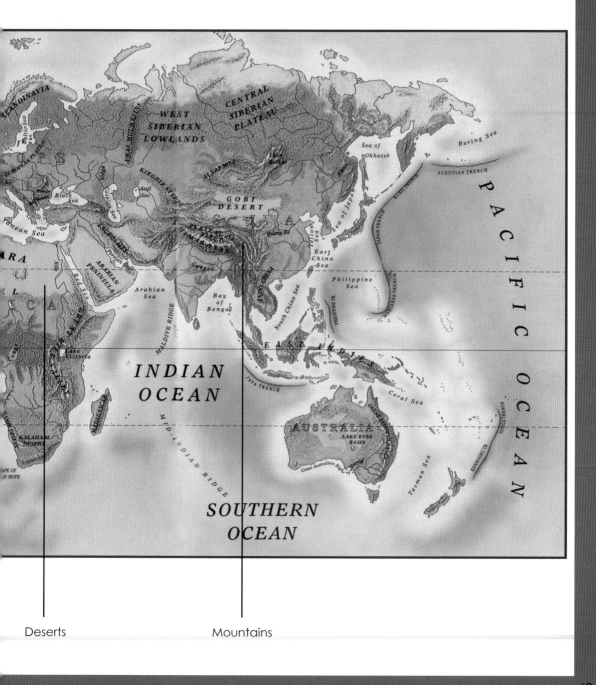

SCANDINAVIA

WEST
SIBERIAN
LOWLANDS

CENTRAL
SIBERIAN
PLATEAU

Bering Sea

Baltic Sea

URAL MOUNTAINS

EUROPEAN PLATEAU

ROPE

Lake
Baikal

ALEUTIAN TRENCH

Carpathians

Black
Sea

Caspian Sea

Aral
Sea

KIRGHIZ STEPPE

ALTAI MTS

Sea of
Okhotsk

GOBI
DESERT

Sea of Japan

KURIL TRENCH

P A C I F I C

SARA

Mediterranean Sea

Persian Gulf

TAKLA MAKAN

Huang He

Yellow
Sea

JAPAN TRENCH

ICA

ARABIAN
PENINSULA

PLATEAU OF
TIBET

Ganges

East
China
Sea

Red Sea

Nile

Arabian
Sea

Bay
of
Bengal

INDO-CHINA

Philippine
Sea

MARIANAS TRENCH

PHILIPPINE TR.

GREAT RIFT VALLEY

Congo

Lake
Victoria

MALDIVE RIDGE

South China Sea

E A S T   I N D I E S

JAVA TRENCH

O C E A N

SUDAN

INDIAN
OCEAN

MADAGASCAR

Coral Sea

BOWERS VALLEY

NAMIB DESERT

KALAHARI
DESERT

M I D - I N D I A N   R I D G E

AUSTRALIA

LAKE EYRE
BASIN

GREAT DIVIDING RANGE

KERMADEC TR

TONGA TRENCH

CAPE OF
GOOD HOPE

Great Australian Bight

Tasman Sea

SOUTHERN
OCEAN

Deserts   Mountains

POLITICAL MAP of the WORLD

These maps can be revised over time as politics and structures change.
This map reflects the countries as they are during one period in time.

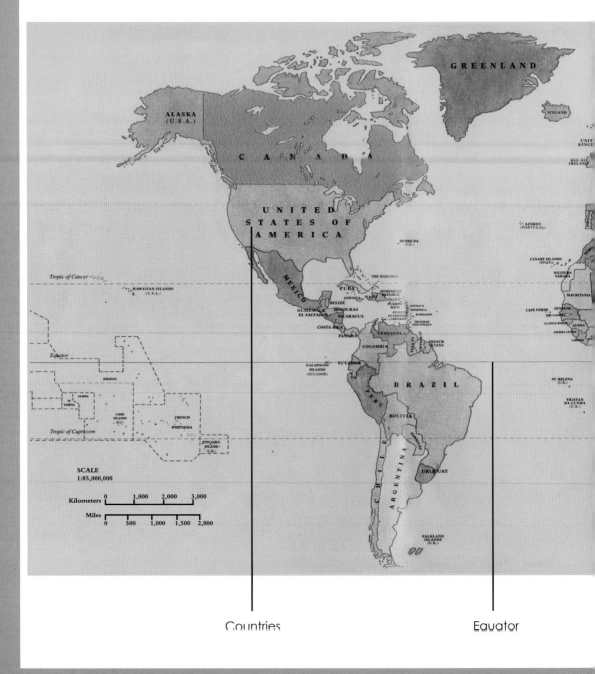

Countries

Equator

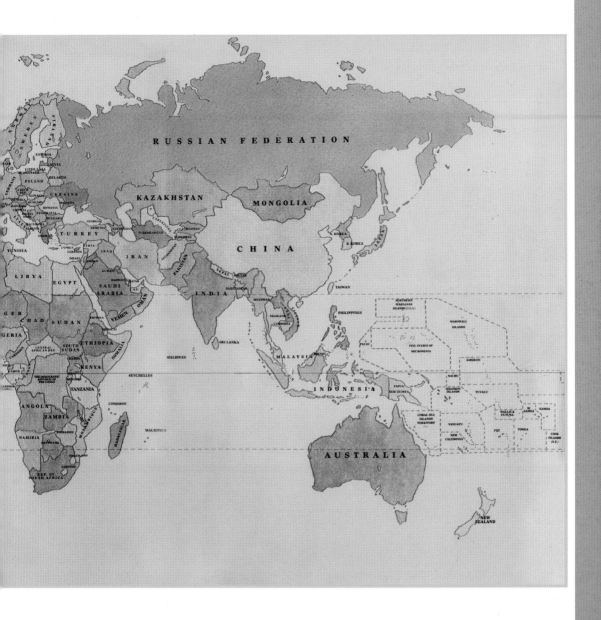

GLOSSARY

Altitude: How high (or low) something is, as compared to the level of the ocean.

Boreal: A cold region dominated by forests of birch, poplar, and conifers.

Climate: The weather conditions in general over a long period of time.

Coniferous: A bush or tree that stays green all year round, such as fir, pine, and spruce trees.

Cultural: The way people live; their ideas, customs, and traditions.

Deciduous: A bush or tree that loses its leaves every year, such as maple, birch, and oak trees.

Economic: The way money, goods, and services are made and used in a society.

Extinct: No longer existing, or having no living members.

Fertile: Able to support the growth of many plants.

Fjord: A long, narrow inlet of the ocean between high cliffs. Fjords were formed by glaciers during the Ice Age.

Geyser: A spring that shoots streams of boiling water and steam up into the air from time to time.

Hemisphere: The earth's surface is divided by the equator into the Northern and Southern Hemispheres.

Industry: Organizing goods or services for people to buy or use.

Inhabit: To live in a place.

Landmass: A continent or other large body of land.

Microscopic: So tiny that it cannot be seen without a microscope.

Monsoon: A very strong wind that blows across the Indian Ocean and southern Asia, bringing rain.

Navigate: To find one's way, especially over a long distance.

Political: Relating to the government or policies of a country.

Prosperous: Having financial success and good fortune.

Rain forest: A dense evergreen forest that has heavy rainfall all year long.

Scavenge: To search for and feed on rotting meat left by other animals.

Surveyor: A person who determines the boundaries and elevations of land or structures.

Taiga: Cold woodland forest areas located in the northern parts of the world.

Tributary: A stream or river that flows into a larger one.

Tundra: A vast, treeless plain in the Arctic regions between the ice cap and the tree line.

Photo Credits
Illustrations by Steven Sweet, Simon Girling & Associates.
Photos from *The Young People's Atlas of the World* except where indicated:

p. 1: windmills of Kinderdijk, jorisvo; Eiffel Tower, majeczka; Forbidden City, Hung Chung Chih; p. 2: St. Peter's, missdragonfly1206; p. 3: CN Tower, rmnoa357; St. Basil, Andrey Starostin; p. 6: globe, Maxx-Studio; p. 8: geyser, Andrea Izzotti; p. 10: Grand Canyon, Christopher Kolaczan; Golden Gate Bridge, turtix; Statue of Liberty, chaiyawat sripimonwan; p. 11: Greenland, Egon NYC; CN Tower, rmnoa357; Niagra Falls, Kevin Tavares; p. 14: Amazon River, JaySi; p. 15: Machu Pichu, ocphoto; Chichen Itza, i-m-a-g-e; Angel Falls, Vadim Petrakov; Middle of the World Monument, KalypsoWorldPhotography; p. 16-17: p. 18: Neuschwanstein Castle, Andreas Zerndl; St. Basil's Cathedral, Andrey Starostin; p. 19: Eiffel Tower, majeczka; Stonehenge, jaroslava V; Little Mermaid, Alan Kraft; Colosseum, Sergiy Zavgorodny; p. 22: Dubai, Posonskyi Andrey; Sahara, CraigBurrows; p. 23: Pyramids, Danita Delmont; Victoria Falls, Przemyslaw Skibinski; Mt. Kilimanjaro, fotoban eos; p. 24: Gobi Desert, hecke61; p. 26: Trans-Siberian Railway, ALEKSANDR RIUTIN; Great Wall, PlusONE; p. 27: Forbidden City, Hung Chung Chih; Mt. Fuji, Sakarin Sawasdinaka; Bullet Train, Thomas Nord; p. 28-29: p. 30: Taj Mahal, happystock; p. 31: Banaue Rice Terraces, Lukasz Kurbiel; Angkor Wat, Tom Roche; Mt. Everest, Kaetana; p. 34: New Guinea Coast, Byelikova Oksana; Ayers Rock, Stanislav Fosenbauer; p. 35: Franz Josef Glacier, Natapong Ratanavi; Mt. Eden Crater, gopixgo; Sydney Opera House, Selfiy; p. 37: Transantarctic Mountains, Sergey Tarasenko; p. 39: arctic fox: Jamen Percy; polar bear, chbaum; snow geese, Robert L Kothenbeutel; p. 44: wolf, Holly Kuchera; pine marten, Mark Caunt; p. 53: Ayers Rock, Stanislav Fosenbauer; Forbidden City, Hung Chung Chih; Angkor Wat, Tom Roche.

LANDMARKS of the WORLD

The landmarks—some of the most recognizable, fascinating, and beautiful places in the world!

1. **Mt. McKinley**—the highest mountain in North America, in Alaska's Denali National Park, with an elevation of 20,237 feet.
2. **Columbia Icefield**—a giant icefield located in the Canadian Rockies and crossing the Continental Divide.
3. **Golden Gate Bridge**—an orange suspension bridge that stretches across the channel between San Francisco Bay and the Pacific Ocean.
4. **Redwood National State Park**—a national park in California, famous for its large sequoia trees that have about a 2,000-year life span.
5. **Chichen Itza**—one of the largest Mayan cities, now located in the Mexican state of Yucatan.
6. **Yellowstone National Park**—this park in Wyoming is home to a cone geyser that erupts approximately every 91 minutes.
7. **Grand Canyon**—a huge canyon in Arizona, 277 miles long, 18 miles wide, and a mile deep!
8. **Gateway Arch**—a 630-foot-high stainless-steel monument in St. Louis, Missouri. It is the tallest man-made monument in the United States, and the world's tallest arch.
9. **Mt. Rushmore**—a sculpture carved into the Black Hills of South Dakota featuring 60-foot sculptures of the faces of four U.S. presidents.
10. **CN Tower**—a 1,814-foot observation tower in Toronto, Canada. It is the largest freestanding structure in the Western Hemisphere.
11. **Statue of Liberty**—a 305-foot statue that stands on Liberty Island in New York Harbor and was a gift from France as a symbol of freedom and friendship.
12. **The White House**—the official residence of the president of the United States of America. It is located in Washington, D.C.
13. **Niagara Falls**—a group of three waterfalls on the border between the United States and Canada.
14. **Galapagos Islands**—volcanic islands off the coast of Ecuador, home to many unique animals, including Galapagos tortoises and land iguanas.
15. **Easter Island Moai**—a group of 887 carved stone statues of human figures created by the Rapa Nui people on the Chilean-Polynesian Easter Island.

16. **Middle of the World City**—a landmark north of Quito, Ecuador, that is said to be precisely at Earth's midpoint.
17. **Machu Picchu**—set of ruins in Peru that was built in the 15th century by the Incan civilization.
18. **Angel Falls**—in the jungles of Venezuela is the world's highest uninterrupted waterfall, at a height of 3,211 feet.
19. **Iguazu Falls**—huge waterfalls located on the border of Argentina and Brazil. The waterfalls are a part of the Iguazu River, which flows through Brazil.
20. **Christ of the Corcovado**—a statue of Jesus Christ in Rio de Janeiro, Brazil, on the mountain of Corcovado.
21. **Casa Rosada**—named for its pink color, this beautiful building is the executive mansion of the president of Argentina.
22. **Perito Moreno Glacier**—a three-mile-wide glacier located in the Patagonia region of Argentina.
23. **Transantarctic Mountains**—a mountain range in Antarctica, stretching more than 3,000 miles, which divides east and west Antarctica.
24. **Alhambra**—meaning "Red Castle," it is a palace in Granada, Andalusia, Spain, so named because of its reddish walls.
25. **Rock of Gibraltar**—a 1,398-foot-high limestone rock located off the southwestern tip of Spain.
26. **Big Ben**—the nickname for the clock in the tower at the north end of the Palace of Westminster in London, England.
27. **Balmoral Castle**—a large working estate in Scotland owned by the British royal family.
28. **Stonehenge**—a prehistoric stone monument in southern England and one of the wonders of the world.
29. **Eiffel Tower**—a 1,063-foot-tall iron-lattice tower in Paris, France. It was named after the engineer Gustave Eiffel, whose company designed and built the tower for the 1889 World's Fair.
30. **St. Peter's Basilica**—located within the Vatican City, it is one of the largest churches in the world.
31. **Colosseum**—a stone amphitheater in Rome, Italy, built during the first century.
32. **Neuschwanstein Castle**—a 19th-century palace located in Bavaria, Germany.
33. **Acropolis**—an ancient stone fortress located on a hill overlooking the city of Athens, Greece.

34. **Little Mermaid Statue**—a bronze statue of a mermaid, based on the fairy tale by Hans Christian Andersen, displayed along the promenade in Copenhagen, Denmark.

35. **Blue Mosque**—more formally the Sultan Ahmed Mosque, it is a historic mosque in Istanbul. It is named for the blue tiles adorning the walls of its interior.

36. **Sumela Monastery**—a Greek Orthodox monastery built on a steep cliff at about 3,900 feet in the Pontic Mountains in Turkey.

37. **Hassan II Mosque**—the seventh-largest mosque in the world, located in Casablanca, Morocco.

38. **Great Pyramid**—481-foot tall pyramid in Giza, Egypt, built by Pharaoh Khufu around 2550 BC.

39. **Sphinx**—rock statue of a mythical creature with a lion's body and a human head on the west bank of the Nile in Giza, Egypt. It is the world's largest statue carved from one stone.

40. **Victoria Falls**—a beautiful waterfall in southern Africa on the border of Zambia and Zimbabwe.

41. **Table Mountain**—a mountain with a flat top (a plateau) located in Cape Town, South Africa.

42. **Mt. Kilimanjaro**—in Tanzania, this mountain is the highest in Africa and the highest freestanding mountain in the world at 19,341 feet above sea level.

43. **Temple Mount**—one of the most important religious sites in the Old City of Jerusalem. It has been used as a religious site for thousands of years.

44. **Petra**—a city in southern Jordan that is famous for its rock-cut architecture, established possibly as early as 312 BC.

45. **Dubai Skyline**—the largest city in the United Arab Emirates, home to hundreds of modern skyscrapers.

46. **Winter Palace**—the main residence of the Russian tsars, this palace is St. Petersburg's most impressive attraction.

47. **St. Basil's Cathedral**—a former church located in Red Square in Moscow, Russia. It is famous for its stunning architecture.

48. **Golden Temple**—formally referred to as the Harmandir Sahib, it is located in Amritsar, Punjab, India. It is a prominent Sikh place of worship.

49. **Taj Mahal**—meaning "crown of palaces," it is a white marble mausoleum located in Agra, Uttar Pradesh, India.

50. **Great Wall of China**—a series of walls made of stone, brick, earth, and wood that were later joined together to provide protection from enemies, while also aiding trade and transportation.

51. **Forbidden City**—in the center of Beijing, China, this was the Chinese emperor's palace for over 500 years.

52. **Mt. Fuji**—an active volcano and the highest mountain in Japan at 12,388 feet tall.

53. **Grand Palace**—a complex of buildings at the heart of Bangkok, Thailand. The palace has been the residence of the kings of Siam (and later Thailand) since 1782.

54. **Angkor Wat**—meaning "temple city," it is a temple complex in Cambodia that was first a Hindu, then subsequently a Buddhist, holy place.

55. **Banaue Rice Terraces**—2,000-year-old rice terraces carved into the mountains of Ifugao by ancestors of the indigenous people, mostly by hand.

56. **Borobudur Temple**—built between 750 and 842, this is the largest Buddhist monument in the world.

57. **Ayers Rock**—also called Uluru, it is a large sandstone rock formation in central Australia that is sacred to the Anagu, the Aboriginal people of the area.

58. **Twelve Apostles**—a collection of limestone rock stacks off the shore of the Port Campbell National Park in Victoria, Australia.

59. **Sydney Opera House**—in Sydney, Australia, it is one of the biggest performing-arts centers in the world.

60. **Mt. Eden Crater**—located on Mt. Eden in Auckland, New Zealand, this majestic bowl-like crater is 160 feet deep.

MODEL ASSEMBLY INSTRUCTIONS

Eiffel Tower

1. Carefully punch out the four pieces.
2. Fold all of the tabs back.
3. Look for the tab labeled 1. Insert tab 1 into slot 1.
4. Continue matching numbered tabs and slots until you have completed one side of the tower (1 to 4).
5. Fold together the tabs labeled 5 to create the point of the tower, and tuck it in the top.
6. Continue matching the numbered tabs to the slots until you have added the other two sides and your tower is complete!

Chichen Itza

1. Carefully punch out the seven pieces.
2. Find the two side pieces and fold each piece in half, and then fold back the tabs.
3. Look for the tab labeled 1. Insert tab 1 into slot 1.
4. Continue matching numbered tabs and slots until you have assembled the base of the temple (1 to 4).
5. Now find the four step pieces and fold back the side panels.
6. Add one set of stairs to each side of the temple by inserting the numbered tabs into the corresponding number slots (5 to 8).
7. Fold the top down and insert tab 9 into slot 9.
8. Find the top of the temple piece and fold the sides down.
9. Insert the tabs into the slots on the top of the temple. Your ancient temple is now complete!

Taj Mahal

1. Carefully punch out the nine pieces.
2. Find the two side pieces and fold each piece along the score lines, and then fold back the tabs.
3. Look for the tab labeled 1. Insert tab 1 into slot 1. Complete the base of the temple by inserting tab 2 into slot 2.
4. Make the center tower by inserting tab 13 into slot 13. Then add the tower roof by curving the sections and matching the tab numbers.
5. Now build the four small towers. First wrap the base into a tower shape and insert the end tabs into the end slots. Then curve the roof sections in and insert the numbered tabs into the corresponding numbered slots.
6. Find the flat roof piece. Insert the center tower in the three slots that are in the center of the roof piece (tabs 17, 18, and 19).
7. Now insert the four small towers, one in each corner.
8. Finally, place the roof on the base by matching the tab and slot numbers (3 to 6). Your Taj Mahal is now complete!